D0435656

ORIENTAL RUGS

COMPILED BY TONY CURTIS

Printed by Apollo Press, Unit 5, Dominion Way, Worthing, Sussex.

INTRODUCTION

Congratulations! You now have in your hands an extremely valuable book. It is one of a series specially devised to aid the busy professional dealer in his everyday trading. It will also prove to be of great value to all collectors and those with goods to sell, for it is crammed with illustrations, brief descriptions and valuations of hundreds of antiques.

Every effort has been made to ensure that each specialised volume contains the widest possible variety of goods in its particular category though the greatest emphasis is placed on the middle bracket of trade goods rather than on those once - in - a - lifetime museum pieces whose values are of academic rather than practical interest to the vast majority of dealers and collectors.

This policy has been followed as a direct consequence of requests from dealers who sensibly realise that, no matter how comprehensive their knowledge, there is always a need for reliable, up-to-date reference works for identification and valuation purposes.

When using your Antiques and their Values to assess the worth of goods, please bear in mind that it would be impossible to place upon any item a precise value which would hold good under all circumstances. No antique has an exactly calculable value; its price is always the result of a compromise reached between buyer and seller, and questions of condition, local demand and the business acumen of the parties involved in a sale are all factors which affect the assessment of an object's 'worth' in terms of hard cash.

In the final analysis, however, such factors cancel out when large numbers of sales are taken into account by an experienced valuer, and it is possible to arrive at a surprisingly accurate assessment of current values of antiques; an assessment which may be taken confidently to be a fair indication of the worth of an object and which provides a reliable basis for negotiation.

Throughout this book, objects are grouped under category headings and, to expedite reference, they progress in price order within their own categories. Where the description states 'one of a pair' the value given is that for the pair sold as such.

ISBN 902921 51 7

Copyright © Lyle Publications 1977

Published by Lyle Publications, Glenmayne, Galashiels, Selkirkshire, Scotland.

CONTENTS

A fine quality Kashan carpet, 11ft.4in. x 8ft.   £680
(King & Chasemore)

An Oriental bordered carpet, the blue field with medallion and floral designs, 9ft.5in. x 5ft.4in.
£100

Mid 17th century Isphanan small carpet, 13ft.6in. x 5ft.10in. £620

Soumak small carpet, 11ft.1in. x 7ft.2in. £750

Peking carpet its indigo field woven with a design of 'A hundred Antiques' 10ft.3in. x6 ft.2in. £900

9

Good Meshed carpet, circa 1930,
13ft.8in. x 10ft.1in.   £950

An Isphanan carpet, the ivory field
with a madder medallion, 11ft.
5 ins. x 7 ft. 6 ins.   £1,000

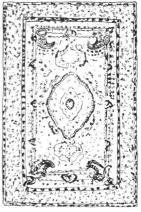

18th century Chinese carpet on an
ivory field, 9ft.6in. x 8ft.1in.£1,700

A finely knotted Kashan carpet,
4.32m. x 3.15m.   £1,800

A fine Teheran carpet of prayer design, 9ft.5in. x 7ft.   £1,850
(King & Chasemore)

A fine, claret ground, Kashan silk carpet, 9ft.3in. x 6ft.4in. £2,000

Chinese carpet, circa 1900,11ft. 6ins. x 13ft.5in.　　　　£2,200

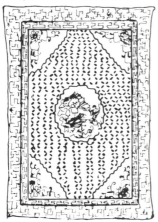

Chinese carpet of about 1770 with pattern of Fo-dogs, in the centre a medallion, 7ft.2in. x 4ft.11in.£2,200

Good Khotan carpet, 14ft.2in. x 7ft.1in.　　　　£2,300

Fine Sile carpet in good condition, 7ft.8in. x 6ft.8in.   £2,400

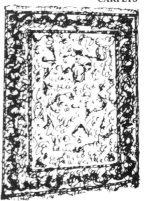

A fine 19th century Tabriz carpet, 12ft. x 9ft.   £2,700

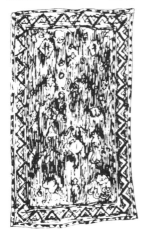

A good carpet from N.W. Persia, with motifs in saffron, green and blue, on a red field, 10ft.10in. x 6ft.   £3,200

Fine 'tree of life' silk Kashan carpet.   £3,200

A fine Isfahan carpet, the ivory field filled with scrolling palmettes and leaves, 13ft.5in. by 10ft.6in.   £3,200

(Sotheby's)

A very fine Tabriz carpet, 18ft.5in. x 12ft.6in. £3,600

A 19th century Sivas mosque carpet, 19ft.10in. x 12ft.7in. £4,200

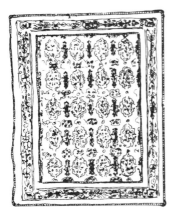

A Mochtachem Kashan carpet with tomato red field, 3.95m. x 3.05m. £5,200

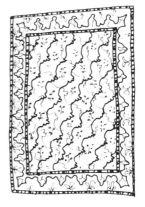

A 16th century North Persian Shrub carpet, 11ft.6in. x 9ft.5in. £62,000

An embroidered Oriental panel. £110
(King & Chasemore)

Bokhara Susani panel, late 19th century, 4ft.6in. x 3ft.6in. £170

Nurata Susani panel, mid 19th century, 7ft.4in. x 5ft.9in. £400

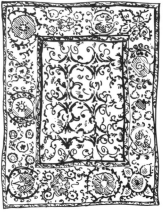

Bokhara Susani panel, late 19th century, 5ft.4in. x 3ft.7in. £400

Susani panel, circa 1860, 8ft.10in. x 7ft. £700

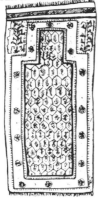

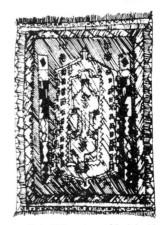

Afshar prayer rug, 5ft.4in. x 2ft.8in.
£28

Early 20th century Afshari double
ended prayer rug, 5ft.11in. x 4ft.
4in.   £50

A Beluch prayer rug, 3ft.6in. x 2ft.
4in.   £85

20th century Roumanian copy of a
Tabriz prayer rug, 5ft.8in. x 4ft.2in.
£100

18

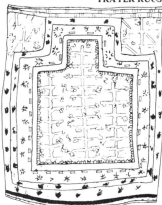

Rare Kuba prayer rug, circa 1820,
4ft.5in. x 2ft.9in.   £110

Beluch prayer rug, 4ft. x 3ft.2in.,
circa 1900.   £160

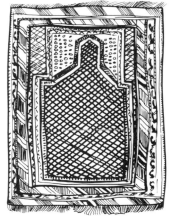

A fine Kashan prayer rug, 4ft.6in.
x 3ft.   £200

Herat Beluchistan prayer rug, 4ft.
7in. x 3ft.6in.   £240

A fine Tabriz prayer rug, 5ft. 8in. x 4ft. 2in.   £275

Modern Kashmir silk prayer rug, 4ft.1in. x 2ft.9in.   £360

Dakhare Qazi Beluchistan prayer rug, circa 1920, 5ft.2in. x 3ft.2in.   £400

Rare Pende prayer rug, circa 1925, 4ft. x 2ft.10in.   £420

An early Bergamo prayer rug, 5ft.2in. x 3ft.6in.   £400
(King & Chasemore)

Kashmir silk prayer rug, 4ft. x 2ft.8in. £430

Daghestan prayer rug, circa 1900, 5ft.9in. x 3ft.10in. £450

A fine Ravar prayer rug. £500

Daghestan prayer rug, 1884, 4ft.7in. x 2ft.11in. £550

A fine old Daghestan prayer rug, 5ft.8in. x 3ft.6in.   £590
(King & Chasemore)

A splendid example of a Hatchli or prayer rug, 5ft.6in. x 4ft.3in.£600

Finely woven Tekke Hatchli prayer rug, 1.44m. x 1.30m.   £640

A Bordjalou Kazak prayer rug, circa 1930, 4ft.5in. x 3ft.8in.   £660

Isphanan prayer rug, circa 1920, 6ft. 4in. x 5ft.   £750

Daghestan prayer rug, 1918, 5ft.
11in. x 5ft. 3in.   £800

Silk Kashan prayer rug, circa 1880,
6ft. 5in. x 4ft. 1in.   £1,150

Turkish Bergama prayer rug, 3ft.
10in. x 3ft. 6in., circa 1800. £1,300

Fachralo Kazak prayer rug, 1916,
4ft. 8in. x 3ft. 5in.   £1,400

25

A fine Daghestan prayer rug, the gold Mihrab with a dark blue
trellis, 4ft.11in. x 3ft.11in.   £1,700
(Sotheby's)

Mid 18th century Ghiordes prayer rug. £2,500

Good Heriz silk prayer rug, 6ft.5in. x 4ft.7in. £3,000

Persian prayer rug, the design featuring a lamp hanging in a crimson panel, the borders decorated with medallion and flower designs, 6ft. x 4ft. £3,600

A silk Tabriz prayer rug with terra cotta Mihrab, 1.79m. x 1.23m. £4,200

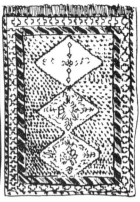

Turkey bordered rug, the blue
field with tree motif, 4ft.10in.
x 4ft.5in.   £12

Caucasian bordered rug, 5ft.6in.
x 3ft.9in.   £20

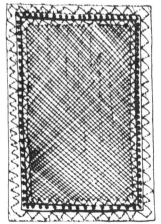

19th century Oriental bordered
rug with small trellis designs on
a fawn field, 4ft.10in. x 3ft.4in.£28

20th century Kelim rug, the field
with three medallions, 4ft.6in. x 2ft.
                             £30

A 19th century Oriental bordered rug with red field decorated with blue trellis design, 5ft.4in. x 3ft.£35

An Indian rug, with cone designs on fawn ground and flower and scroll border, 6ft.9in. x 5ft.6in.   £35

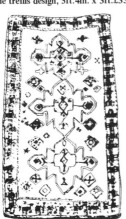

Eastern bordered rug, 6ft.6in. x 3ft.9in.   £38

Eastern bordered rug, 6ft. x 4ft.3in.   £50

Early 20th century Shiraz, 5ft.
11in. x 5ft.   £50

Caucasian bordered rug, 7ft.5in.
x 4ft.10in.   £50

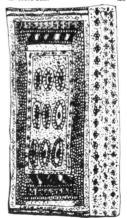

Eastern bordered rug, 4ft.8in.
x 3ft.9in.   £52

Bokhara rug, crimson and blue
ground, bordered, 6ft. x 4ft.1in.
                              £55

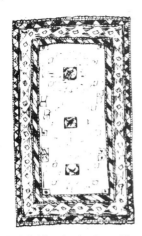

An Asia Minor bordered rug with medallion designs on a blue field, 5ft.4in. x 3ft.5in. £55

A Victorian Oriental bordered rug, the red field with large medallion and geometric designs, 6ft. 10in. x 4ft.3in. £55

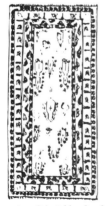

19th century Oriental bordered rug with medallions, 5ft.8in. x 3ft.2in. £58

An interesting Lur tribal rug, circa 1800, 4ft. x 3ft.5in. £60

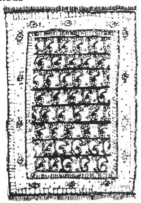

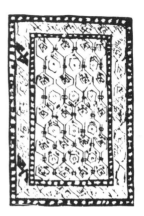

Early 20th century Sehna rug,
6ft.9in. x 4ft.4in.   £60

An Asia Minor bordered rug,
with medallion designs on a
white field, 4ft.6in. x 3ft.3in. £65

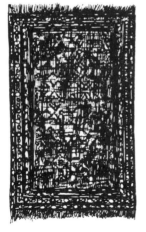

A Fereghan bordered rug with
Herati design on a blue field,
6ft.6in. x 3ft.9in.   £65

Derbend rug, 5ft.11in. x 3ft.9in.
£70

A 19th century Oriental bordered rug with red ground decorated with fine lozenge medallions, 6ft. x 2ft. 9in. £70

A Caucasian bordered rug, the red field with hooked borders, and blue spandrels with medallion designs, 6ft.5in. x 4ft.5in. £75

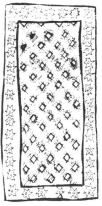

Antique Chinese rug in tones of Imperial blue, 7ft.8in. x 5ft.4½in. £75

An Old Kazak rug, 5ft.5in. x 2ft. 5in. £75

33

19th century Kirman Afshar rug, with three typical Afshari borders, 6ft.5in. x 5ft. £85

A Persian rug with trees and flowers, on ivory field with red floral border, 6ft.7in. x 4ft.11in. £90

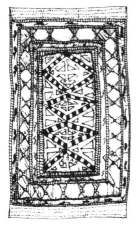

20th century Kazak Genje rug, 5ft. 7in. x 3ft.5in. £95

An Oriental bordered rug, the blue field with pear designs, 5ft. x 3ft. 11in. £95

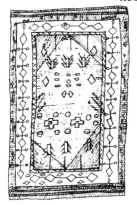

20th century Gashgai rug, 6ft.11in.
x 5ft.   £100

19th century Gashgai rug, 8ft.10in.
x 5ft.4in.   £100

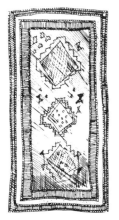

19th century Kazak rug, the field
of three stepped medallions, 6ft.
7in. x 3ft.11in.   £100

Early 20th century Afshar rug,
5ft.1in. x 4ft.   £100

Early 20th century Hamadan rug,
6ft.5in. x 4ft.6in. £100

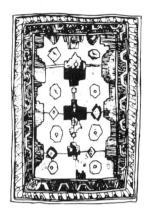

19th century Caucasus Kazakstan
rug, 7ft.7in. x 4ft.1in. £105

Caucasian bordered rug, 5ft.5in.
x 4ft. £105

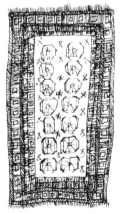

Early 20th century Afghan rug of
the Chub Bash, 7ft.6in. x 5ft.3in.
£105

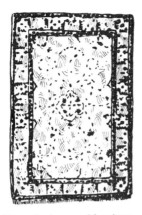

Kirman Persian rug, with an ivory, blue and rose ground, 2m. x 140cm. £110

Persian Kurdistan rug, 7ft. x 4ft.3in., circa 1930. £110

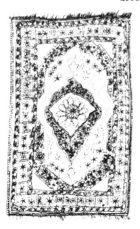

19th century Tabriz rug, 4ft.7in. x 3ft.2in. £130

Eastern bordered rug, 6ft.6in. x 4ft.3in. £130

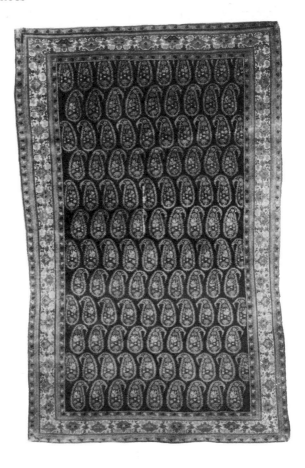

A fine Malayer Hamadan rug, 6ft.8in. x 4ft.3in.　　£130
(King & Chasemore)

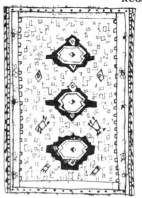

Afshar Shiraz rug, circa 1900, 5ft.
10in. x 4ft.3in. £140

19th century Seichur Soumak rug,
the field of three massive and three
subsidiary medallions, 6ft. x 4ft.
4in. £145

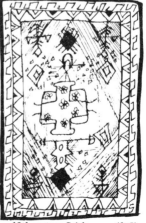

Late 19th century Old Chinese rug,
1.22m. x 0.66m. £150

19th century Seichur rug, 4ft.5in.
x 3ft.1in. £150

Late 19th century Old Chinese rug,
1.22m. x 0.64m.   £150

Early 20th century Yumud of
good colour, 5ft.2in. x 4ft.7in.£150

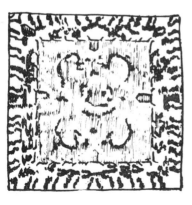

Late 18th century Chinese rug.£150

Late 19th century Old Chinese rug,
1.22m. x 0.66m.   £150

A Teheran rug, the central medallion supported by scattered floral sprays to an ivory ground, 7ft.2in. x 4ft.9in.   £150
(King & Chasemore)

An antique Bergama rug, 5ft.11in. x 4ft.4in.   £165
(King & Chasemore)

An early 19th century Manuluka
rug, 6ft. x 4ft.   £165

A Bessarabian Kelim rug, 9ft. 9in.
x 7ft. 7in.   £165

Early 20th century Tekke rug,
4ft. 6in. x 4ft. 3in.   £165

Mid 19th century East Persian
antique Beluch rug, 1.87m. x
1.09m.   £180

43

Mid 19th century East Persian antique Belouch rug, 1.80m. x 0.98m.

£180

(Rippon and Boswell)

A Tekke Bokhara rug, 100in. x
55in.   £180

Fine Afghan Tekke, circa 1880,
5ft.11in. x 3ft.4in.   £190

A Tekke rug of classical design,
4ft. x 3ft.3in.   £195

Late 19th century central
Persian Old Hamadan rug, 2.90m.
x 1.19m.   £200

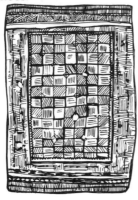

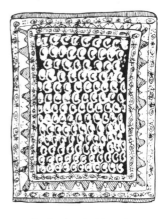

Mid 19th century East Persian
antique Beluch rug, 1.20m. x
0.90m.   £200

Persian Tribal Afshar, 5ft. x
4ft., circa 1880.   £205

Mid 19th century East Persian
antique Beluch rug, 1.33m. x
0.83m.   £220

Late 19th century East Persian
Old Beluch rug, 1.17m. x 0.91m.
                                   £220

Mid 19th century East Persian antique Beluch rug, 1.18m. x 0.90m.
£220

(Rippon and Boswell)

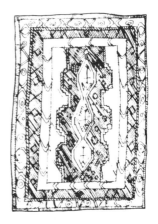

19th century Caucasian Eagle
Kasak rug. £220

A good Gashgai Shiraz rug, 9ft.8in.
x 7ft.1in. £225

Early 20th century Kashan rug,
with a classical Isphanan design,
6ft.5in. x 4ft.1in. £230

Qum hunting rug, 6ft.5in. x 4ft.6in.
£240

Late 19th century central Persian Old Hamadan rug, 1.40m. x 1.07m.
£250
(Rippon and Boswell)

Late 19th century East Persian Old Beluch rug, 2.10m. x 1.19m. £250
(Rippon and Boswell)

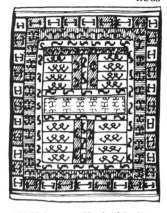

Unusual Erivan rug, circa 1920,
5ft.10in. x 3ft.10in.   £250

Mid 19th century North Afghanistan
antique Afghan Hatchli rug, 1.94m.
x 1.54m.   £250

Karadagh rug, circa 1930, 9ft.3in. x
5ft.   £250

A Derbend rug, circa 1920, 4ft.6in.
x 4ft.   £250

Early 20th century Kashan rug, the central field medallion amid interlacing arabesques, 6ft.3in. x 4ft.3in. £265

Khamseh Shiraz rug, circa 1920, 8ft.9in. x 6ft.4in. £280

Persian Tribal Shiraz, 5ft.8in. x 3ft.5in., circa 1890. £290

Caucasian Soumak, 6ft.11in. x 5ft., circa 1880. £290

A blue ground Erivan rug, 5ft.9in. x 4ft.4in.   £290
(King & Chasemore)

A Tabriz rug having a rose and ivory field with a large pole medallion to the centre field, 6ft.9in. x 4ft. £290
(King and Chasemore)

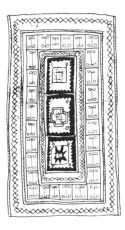

Caucasian Kasak, 6ft.5in. x 3ft.8in.,
circa 1880.   £300

Kuba Kabistan rug, circa 1890, 6ft.
3in. x 4ft.6in.   £300

Late 19th century South Persian
Old Shiraz Kelim rug, 2.08m. x
1.42m.   £310

Fine Isphanan\rug, with multi
colour floral design, on white
ground, 7ft.5in. x 4ft.10in.£310

An Isphanan¹ rug, the central rose pole medallion edged in blue strapwork, 7ft. x 4ft.7in.   £315

Kashan rug, circa 1930, 7ft.2in. x 4ft.5in.   £320

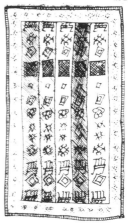

Late 19th century central Persian Old Mossul Hamadan rug, 2.06m. x 1.45m.   £320

A rare Armenian Kazak rug, dated 1800, 6ft.9in. x 3ft.8in.   £320

A Tekke Turkoman | Ensi, the quarter field containing ram's horns, circa
1900, 4ft.11in. x 4ft.4in.   £320
(Sotheby's)

A fine Saruk rug with a pole medallion to the centre field supported by small vase, rosette and floral spray designs, 6ft.4in. x 4ft.2in.   £340
(King & Chasemore)

A Persian rug with centre medallion
and corners, white ground with red
pattern border, 7ft.4in. x 4ft.7in.
£340

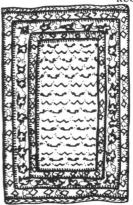

Mid 19th century South Persian
antique Afshar rug, 1.64m. x 1.16m.
£350

Rare Tashkent shaped horse rug,
circa 1850, 5ft.11in. x 4ft.5in. £360

Armenian Kazak rug, dated 1890,
7ft. x 4ft.3in. £360

A fine Kashan picture rug, the central medallion depicting a Middle-Eastern landscape, 6ft.8in. x 4ft.6in.   £360
(King & Chasemore)

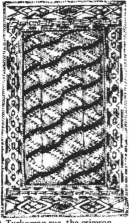

A Turkoman rug, the crimson ground with four rows of rectangular medallions, the primary borders with hook designs, 8ft. x 4ft. 8in. £360

A magnificent Shirvan rug, the field with a geometric version of the Fakteh Jamshid, circa 1910. £375

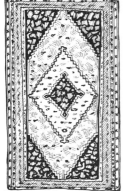

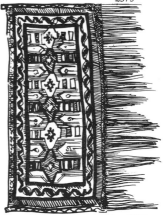

A Sennen Kelim rug, the madder field with a diamond ivory pole medallion, 6 ft. 7 ins. x 4 ft. 4 ins., circa 1900 £400

Yumud Chahrchango rug, circa 1880, 4ft. 6in. x 1ft. 8in. £400

Mid 19th century central Anatolian antique Kirshehir rug, 1.61 m. x 0.99 m. £400

Kurdish rug, circa 1912, 7 ft. 6 in. x 4 ft. £400

Turkoman Beshire, 6 ft. 8 in. x 4 ft., circa 1900. £405

A Turkoman rug, 84 in. x 48 in. £410

A fine Malayer Hamadan rug, 7ft.3in. x 4ft.5in.   £410
(King & Chasemore)

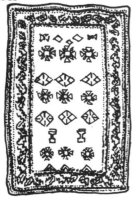

Antique Caucasian 'Fertility' rug,
6ft. 3in. x 4ft. 3in.   £425

Tekke Turkoman rug, circa 1880,
5ft. 8in. x 5ft. 2in.   £440

Mid 19th century South Russian
antique Yumud rug, 1.37m. x
0.91m.   £450

Early 20th century North-East
Persian Old Yumud rug, 1.95m.
x 1.37m.   £450

Mid 19th century East Persian antique Beluch rug, 1.22m. x 0.68m. £450
(Rippon and Boswell)

Late 19th century South Persian Shiraz rug, 1.62m. x 1.25m.   £450
(Rippon and Boswell)

Mid 19th century South Persian
antique Shiraz rug, 1.76m. x
1.29m.   £450

Antique Kirman laver rug, circa
1840, 6ft.1in. x 4ft.1in.   £450

Hila-Kuba rug, circa 1870, 4ft.4in.
x 3ft.5in.   £480

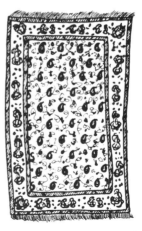

Modern Qum rug, 6ft.7in. x 4ft.
7in.   £480

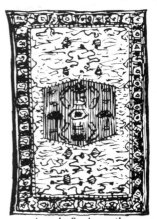

Nomadic Kazak rug, circa 1900, 7ft. 6in. x 4ft.7in. £500

An early Saruk rug, the cream woven field with a large terra cotta medallion, 6ft.11in. x 4ft.1in. £525

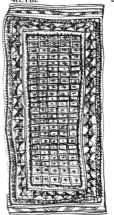

Antique Peking rug, late 19th century, 7ft.1in. x 4ft.4in. £540

Late 19th century East Persian Old Beluch rug, 3.31m. x 1.56m. £540

A fine Kashan rug, the rust coloured field extensively decorated with floral sprays, 7ft.3in. x 4ft.5in.   £540

(King & Chasemore)

Mid 19th century South Persian
antique Shiraz rug, 1.88m. x 1.29m.
£550

Shirvan rug, 117cm. x 94cm. £550

Late 19th century South Persian
Old Shiraz rug, 2.08m. x 1.47m.
£550

Mid 19th century South Persian
antique Afshar rug, 2.02m. x 1.68m.
£600

A Neriz rug with an indigo field and ivory spandrels filled with a Boteh and flower heads design, 8ft.3in. x 4ft.9in., circa 1870. £600

A Boulevadi Shiraz rug, the indigo field with three triple pole medallions, circa 1920, 7ft.7in. x 5ft. £600

A Qashqai Kelim, the madder field with zig-zag guls in saffron, circa 1880, 9ft.11in. x 4ft.7in. £600

Late 19th century South Persian old figured Kirman rug, 0.72m. x 0.60m. £600

71

A fine white ground Tabriz rug, 8ft.6in. x 5ft.6in.   £600
(King & Chasemore)

Early 20th century central Anatolian
Old Panderma rug, 1.73m. x 1.24m.
£600

Mid 19th century South Persian
antique Afshar rug, 1.62m. x 1.28m.
£600

Mid 19th century South Persian
antique Shiraz rug, 2.35m. x 1.67m.
£600

Yumud rug, circa 1900, 5ft.10in.
x 3ft.10in. £620

Late 19th century South Russian Old Pende rug, 1.32m. x 0.89m. £650
(Rippon and Boswell)

A very fine Isphanan|rug, 7ft.2in.
x 4ft.9in.   £700

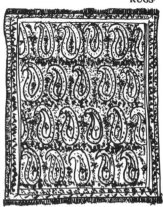

Mid 19th century Persian rug
showing the boteh motif.£700

Early 20th century North-West
Persian Old Tabriz rug, 1.94m. x
1.37m.   £700

Late 19th century central
Persian antique Sameni rug,
3.61m. x 1.56m.   £700

Early 19th century Armenian
Kazak rug, 6ft.10in. x 5ft.1in.
£725

Mid 19th century central Persian
antique Hamadan rug, 2.02m. x
1.28m.   £750

Early 20th century central Persian
Old Senneh Hamadan rug, 1.93m.
x 1.32m.   £750

One of a pair of modern Kashmir
rugs, 6ft.10in. x 5ft.   £750

Central Persian Old Isphanan rug, circa 1900, 2.20m. x 1.41m.   £750
(Rippon and Boswell)

A Chinese silk antique rug, 8ft.6in. x 6ft.3in.   £750
(King & Chasemore)

An antique Neriz rug. £750

Mid 19th century South Persian
antique Neriz rug, 1.83m. x 1.16m.
£750

Persian Kirman rug, 7ft.6in. x 5ft.
circa 1890. £775

Mid 19th century central Persian
antique Bijar rug, 2.01m. x 1.27m.
£800

A rare Waziri rug, the walnut and ivory field with three bands of madder S's and two medallions, circa 1920, 5ft.3in. x 3ft.1in.   £860
(Sotheby's)

A Kashan rug with a central medallion and floral sprays in pale blue and ivory on a wine red field, 6ft.7in. x 4ft.4in.   £880

Tekke Ensi Turkoman rug, circa 1880, 4ft.8in. x 4ft.   £900

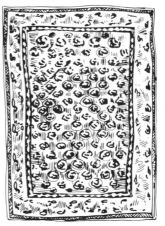

Late 19th century South Persian Old Kirman rug, 2.29m. x 1.42m.   £900

Late 19th century Old Derbend rug, 2.93m. x 1.64m.   £900

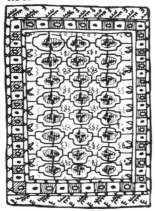

Late 19th century South Russian
Old Bokhara rug, 1.90m. x 1.35m.
£900

Early 20th century central Persian
Old Figural Kashan rug, 2.00m.
x 1.31m. £900

Late 19th century central Persian
Old Isphanan rug, 2.08m. x 1.37m.
£900

A good Fereghan rug with a central
medallion and floral decoration, 6ft.
2in. x 4ft.1in. £900

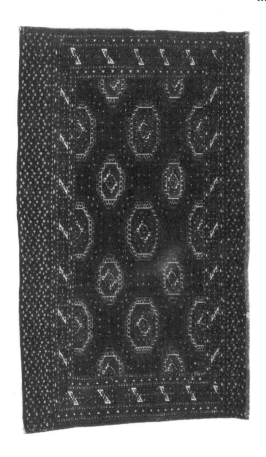

A Pende Juval rug with seven free standing guls centred in silk, circa 1850, 3ft.4in. x 5ft.9in. £900

(Sotheby's)

**Mid 19th century Anatolian antique Panderma rug, 1.43m. x 1.24m. £950
(Rippon and Boswell)**

A fine Kashan rug, 4ft.9in. x
7ft.10in.   £950

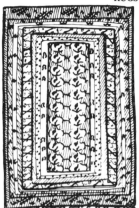

Late 19th century South Russian
Old Tekke Turkoman rug, 1.91m.
x 1.23m.   £950

Late 19th century Shirvan rug, 7ft.
2in. x 4ft.7in.   £950

Chinese rug about 1850, 9ft.3in.
x 6ft.1in., with a dragon motif in
brown on a blue field.   £950

One of a pair of Kashan rugs, circa 1930, 6ft.9in. x 4ft.4in.   £950

Tekke rug, circa 1870, in the traditional colours and design of a Bokhara.   £950

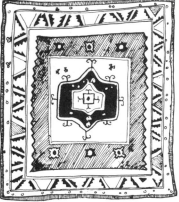

Caucasian Kazak, 4ft.6in. x 4ft.1in., circa 1850.   £1,000

A Shirvan Chi Chi rug the indigo field filled with guls and stars, 6ft. 6ins. x 4ft. 1in.   £1,000

A fine pair of Isphanan rugs, 84in. x 54in.　　　　£1,000
(King & Chasemore)

A fine Kashan antique rug, 6ft.9in. x 4ft.3in.   £1,000
(King & Chasemore)

Mid 19th century Peking rug, 6ft. 10in. x 4ft.6in., in good condition. £1,000

Mid 19th century antique Kazak rug, 2.05m. x 1.15m.   £1,000

Fine Kazak-Chelabird rug, circa 1880, 8ft.9in. x 4ft.6in.   £1,050

Unusual Yumud Ensi Turkoman rug, circa 1880, 5ft.2in. x 4ft.4in.   £1,050

A superb antique silk Kashan rug, 6ft.8in. x 4ft.4in.　£1,050
(King & Chasemore)

Fine modern Nain rug, 5ft.6in. x
3ft.9in.   £1,100

Early 20th century North-West
Persian Old Tabriz rug, 2.05m.
x 1.40m.   £1,100

Early 20th century South Russian
Old Bokhara rug, 1.85m. x 1.50m.
                            £1,100

Late 19th century Old Karabagh
rug, 4.10m. x 1.30m.   £1,150

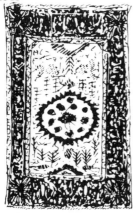

A rare Fereghan rug of Mustafiz design, centred by a medallion and surrounded by characteristic stylised floral motifs, 6ft.8in. x 4ft. 6in. £1,200

19th century Qashgai rug in shades of brick red, blue, brown and white. £1,200

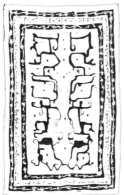

Persian Heriz rug, 7ft.4in. x 5ft. 3in., circa 1850. £1,200

Late 19th century Old Shirvan rug, 3.43m. x 1.44m. £1,200

A fine Kashan picture rug depicting the story of Joseph, the border
with verses from Persian poets and portraits of Persian Kings, 8ft.
x 4ft.6in.   £1,220

(King & Chasemore)

Mid 19th century antique Dagestan
rug, 1.36m. x 1.00m.   £1,220

Early 19th century antique Beshir
rug, 7ft.7in. x 4ft.7in.   £1,250

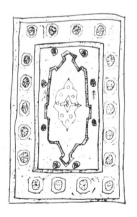

North-West Persian rug.   £1,300

Late 19th century South Russian
Old Yumud Hatchli rug, 1.64m.
x 1.32m.   £1,300

A Teheran rug, 6ft.6in. x 5in.
£1,350

A Tabriz silk rug, having the characteristically regular design, soft shades and coarse weave, 5ft.3in. x 4ft.1in.   £1,400

Kashan silk rug, 6ft.5in. x 4ft.4in.
£1,400

Late 19th century central Persian Old Kashan rug, 1.95m. x 1.34m.
£1,400

One of a pair of Kashan rugs, 6ft. 10in. x 4ft.9in. £1,400

Fine Isphanan rug with cream field and rust border, 7ft.4in. x 4ft.9in. £1,500

Caucasian Kuba, 5ft.10in. x 3ft. 6in., circa 1850. £1,500

Chondzoresk Kazak rug, circa 1900, excellent condition, 6ft.10in. x 4ft. 9in. £1,550

Silk Persian Qum hunting rug, 5ft.3in. x 6ft.6in.   £1,600

A rare Salor rug, the madder field divided by a band of minor guls,
circa 1900, 5ft.4in. x 3ft.6in.   £1,600
(Sotheby's)

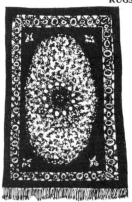

Persian Quash Gai, 5ft.6in. x 3ft. 8in., circa 1870.   £1,600

Good quality Isphanan rug. £1,600

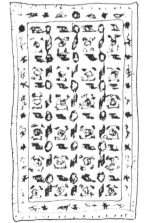

Asia Minor rug with 17th century design on a predominantly ivory ground, 8ft.7in. x 5ft.   £1,600

Late 19th century Old Leshgi rug, 2.90m. x 1.14m.   £1,600

Mid 19th century antique Shirvan
rug, 3.10m. x 1.19m.   £1,600

Akstafa Shirvan rug, circa 1880,
8ft.2in. x 3ft.11in.   £1,800

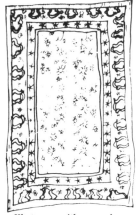

Khotan rug with vase and
pomegranate type design
12ft. 4 in. x 5ft.10 in. £1,800

Mid 19th century antique Kazak
rug, 2.70m. x 1.13m.   £1,800

A Shirvan rug, the terra cotta field with a design of stylised lilies, leaves, flowerheads and jewellery, 5ft.10in. x 4ft.10in. £1,900
(Sotheby's)

Kuba rug, circa 1870, 5ft.11in. x 4ft. £2,000

Early 20th century central Persian Old Kashan rug, 2.07m. x 1.34m. £2,000

A good Kashan rug, woven with a red central medallion on a blue and ivory field, 7ft.2in. x 4ft.6in. £2,200

Fine part silk Isphanan/rug with floral surrounds, 7ft.8in. x 4ft.11in. £2,250

Mid 19th century central Anatolian antique Bergama rug, 1.93m. x 1.45m.
£2,500

Tabriz picture rug with central picture lozenge, 10ft.3in. x 6ft.2in.
£2,500

Late 19th century central Persian Old Teheran rug, 2.14m. x 1.17m.
£2,500

One of a pair of Kashan silk rugs, 6ft.10in. x 4ft.6in.   £2,600

An Akstafa rug, the madder field with three major guls and eight
peacocks with botehs, circa 1880, 10ft. x 4ft.4in.   £2,800
(Sotheby's)

Late 19th century central Persian
Old Teheran rug, 1.92m. x 1.40m.
£3,000

Late 19th century central Persian
Old Teheran rug, 2.11m. x 1.45m.
£3,000

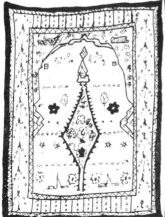

Persian Heriz, 7ft.2in. x 5ft.6in.,
circa 1850.   £3,400

A very fine Kashan silk rug, 10ft. x
6ft.   £3,400

Late 19th century central Persian silk Old Isphanan rug, 2.08m. x 1.35m. £3,500

One of a pair of fine wool Kashan picture rugs, 54in. x 83in. £4,000

Antique Karatchoph Kazak rug, circa 1900, 7ft.5in. x 5ft.1in. £4,000

One of a pair of silk Kashan rugs, the ivory field with a madder medallion and indigo spandrels, circa 1920. £4,000

Silk Tabriz rug with terra cotta
mihrab, 1.79m. x 1.23m. £4,200

One of a pair of Tabriz pictorial
rugs, the rose field with a medallion
containing a scene of a river, ducks,
deer and a doe, circa 1940. £4,200

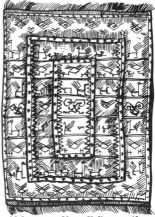

Fine Seichur rug, 19th century,
9ft.10in. x 5ft.3in.   £4,400

19th century Verne Kelim rug, 6ft.
6in. x 5ft.   £4,800

A rare Kashan silk embossed rug, decorated with portraits of great men of history within borders of Arabic numerals. £5,000

One of a pair of antique Kashan pictorial rugs, 6ft.7in. x 4ft.4in., circa 1870. £5,000

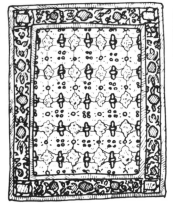

A large Mochtachem Kashan rug, 3.95m. x 3.05m.£5,200

20th century central Persian silk Qum rug, 2.76m. x 1.85m.£6,000

A fine embossed silk Kashan｜rug, the pale aubergine ground filled with flowering and foliate stems, 6ft. 8in. x 4ft. 3in. £6,500
(Henry Spencer and Sons)

An antique silk Heriz rug, the rust coloured field decorated with
stylised floral and scroll motifs, 5ft.9in. x 4ft.8in.　　£7,800
(King & Chasemore)

Mid 19th century North-West
Persian antique silk Heriz rug, 1.88m.
x 1.37m. £6,500

One of a pair of antique Kashan
rugs, the ivory field with a pole
medallion and spandrels, all filled
with flowers, 6ft.5in. x 4ft.3in.,
circa 1840. £7,000

A silk Hereke rug woven partly with
a silver thread on wine red field.
£7,200

17th century Kashan Kelim rug.
£58,000

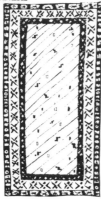

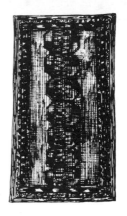

A central Asian bordered runner with coloured diagonal striped field and hooked design, 7ft.8in. x 3ft. 6in.   £25

A Turkoman bordered runner, the red ground with row of six octagons, 8ft. x 4ft.5in.   £35

An Oriental bordered runner, the red field with pear design, 7ft.6in. x 3ft.2in.   £40

19th century Genje runner, 9ft.9in. x 3ft.2in.   £50

An Indian bordered runner of Persian design, the dark field with multi-coloured medallions, 9ft.6in. x 4ft.3in. £80

Large Afghan runner rug, 216in. x 42in., on a red ground. £145

Late 19th century South Russian old Turkoman tent band, 1.02m. x 0.40m. £200

Seichur antique runner, 10ft.8in. x 3ft.8in. £360

113

Kazak Bordjalou runner, circa 1880, 8ft.3in. x 3ft.2in. £620

Fine Saliani Baku runner, circa 1880, 11ft.10in. x 3ft.11in. £820

A Moghan runner, the indigo field with nine hooked guls, 9ft.8in. x 4ft., circa 1840. £1,000

A Moghan runner, the indigo field with four oblong medallions and four guls, 8ft.8in. x 4ft., dated 1275 AH. £1,050

An extremely fine, semi antique Shirvan runner, 14ft.6in. x 4ft.1in. £1,100

A Talish runner, the main indigo field with a boteh design, 9ft.6in. x 3ft.10in., circa 1800. £1,100

Rare Chi-Chi runner, 2.84m. x 1.35m. £1,400

Fine antique Kabistan runner, circa 1850, 12ft.4in. x 5ft. £1,400

SADDLE BAGS

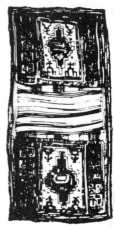

A pair of old Persian Beluch saddle bags. £20

A modern pair of Persian saddle bags. £25

A small Turkoman Beluch saddle bag. £70

Pendic Bokhara half saddle bag. £95

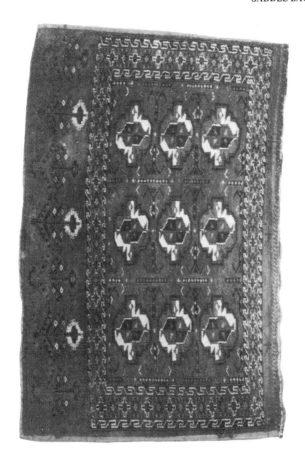

A Yumud Bokhara half saddle bag.   £95
·(King & Chasemore)

Late 19th century East Persian Old Beluch saddle bag, 2.48m. x 0.60m. £160

Tekke saddle bag, circa 1900, 3ft. 5in. x 1ft. 7in. £170

Yumud Turkman saddle bag, circa 1900, 3ft. 8in. x 1ft. 6in. £170

19th century Sehna Rupalani (bride's dowry saddle cover), 3ft. 5in. x 3ft. 2in. £200

Mid 19th century East Persian antique Belouch saddle bag, 1.04m. x 0.65m. £220

Mongol saddle rug, 1.27m. x 61cm. £399

A splendid example of a finely woven Yumud Osmolduk or animal trapping, 4ft. 3ins. wide. £650

Yumud horse cover with cane design on a madder field in indigo, pomegranate, natural and walnut. £750

119

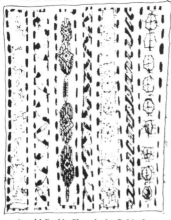

An old Beshir Choval, the field of
Ersari guls laid in horizontal stripes
(damaged) 4ft.10in. x 3ft.10in.£20

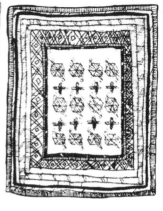

An old Tekke Choval, 4ft.10in. x
3ft.2in.   £35

A Persian pillow with pile cover.£40

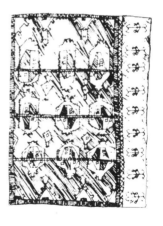

An interesting Tekke Choval (tent
bag) 4ft.2in. x 2ft.10in.   £60

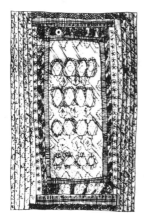

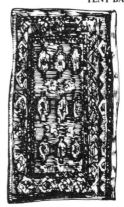

19th century Saruk Choval (tent bag complete with back), 5ft.9in. x 3ft. 7in. £75

A complete storage bag with an unusual skirt, made by the Tekke, 5ft.4in. x 3ft.7in. £130

A bag face by the Ersari Beshir tribe, with chevron design, 4ft.8in. x 3ft. £240

A Turkoman storage bag face with simple geometric design, 2ft.8in. x 4ft.1in. £240

Mid 19th century South Persian antique Quashgai bag, 0.61 m. x 0.61 m.
£300
(Rippon and Boswell)

INDEX